# STICKER ENCYCLOPEDIA

# THINGS THAT GO

# About this book

## REVISED EDITION

**Assistant Editor** Agey George
**Project Editor** Robin Moul
**Senior Editor** Roohi Sehgal
**US Editor** Jane Perlmutter
**US Senior Editor** Shannon Beatty
**Assistant Art Editor** Nishtha Gupta
**Art Editors** Mohd Zishan, Eleanor Bates
**Senior Art Editor** Kanika Kalra
**Managing Editors** Monica Saigal, Penny Smith
**Managing Art Editor** Ivy Sengupta
**DTP Designers** Dheeraj Singh, Syed Md Farhan
**Assistant Picture Researcher** Mamta Panwar
**Jacket Designer** Rashika Kachroo
**Production Editor** Becky Fallowfield
**Senior Production Controller** Ena Matagic
**Delhi Creative Heads** Glenda Fernandes, Malavika Talukder
**Deputy Art Director** Mabel Chan
**Publishing Director** Sarah Larter

## ORIGINAL EDITION

**Written by** Phil Hunt
**Consultant** Bob Woods
**Editor** Marie Greenwood
**Art Editor** Polly Appleton, Chloe Luxford
**Design Development Manager** Helen Senior
**Publishing Manager** Becky Hunter
**Associate Publisher** Sue Leonard
**Production Editor** Laragh Kedwell
**Production** Nick Seston
**Picture Researcher** Harriet Mills
**Jacket Designer** Victoria Harvey

## HOW TO USE THIS BOOK

Read the information pages, and then search for the relevant stickers in the back of the book to fill in the spaces. Use the sticker outlines and labels to help you.

There are lots of extra stickers that you can use to decorate the scenes at the back of the book. It's up to you where you put them all. The most important thing is to have lots of sticker fun!

# Contents

# Animal power

Before automobiles or trains, people traveled in carriages pulled by animals. Journeys were slow, but passengers could travel long distances in a covered stagecoach or across town in a horse-drawn cab or bus.

## CHARIOT

In Roman times, men raced against each other in a special cart called a chariot, pulled by two or more horses. The races were fast and dangerous.

## STAGECOACH

Before trains, people traveled across country in a stagecoach. Up to eight passengers sat inside the coach, while their luggage was strapped to the top.

## HANSOM CAB

In London, Paris, and New York, in the 1800s, the hansom cab was the fastest way of traveling around the city. The driver steered the horse from behind the cab.

## HORSE-DRAWN BUS

A horse-drawn bus was pulled by two large horses, and carried up to 24 passengers. People climbed stairs to reach the top deck or sat in the covered deck below.

## OXCART

Since ancient times, the oxcart has been used to transport goods and people. The driver sits in the front of the cart, while goods are loaded in the back.

## DOGSLED

A dogsled is pulled by dogs, usually Alaskan huskies, and travels on snow and ice. The sled slides on blades called runners.

# Bicycles

A bicycle is a human-powered vehicle with two wheels attached to a frame. It is a very popular way of getting around.

### High-wheel bike

The high-wheel, also called a penny-farthing, was the first bike invented. To mount it, the rider used a small peg near the back wheel to climb on.

### Tandem bike

A tandem is designed for two people to ride at the same time. It has two seats, and two sets of pedals, brakes, and handlebars.

### Road bike

Built for traveling long distances in comfort, a road bike has gears and brakes to help the rider go up and down steep hills.

### Electric bike

An electric bike comes with a battery and an electric motor. It can travel long distances faster and more easily than a normal bicycle.

### Recumbent bike

These bikes are faster and more comfortable than an upright bicycle. A recumbent bike has a wide seat and backrest that allows riders to cycle in a laid-back position.

# Motorcycles

A motorcycle is a two-wheeled vehicle powered by an engine. While some are better for short distances, others can cruise along highways for miles.

## Quad bike

A quad bike is a motorcycle with four chunky tires. These bikes are usually not allowed on streets, but they're a lot of fun for off-road riding.

## Sports bike

A sports bike is designed for speed on the street and the racetrack. It has a powerful engine and light parts, such as its wheels and frame.

## Moped

A moped is a motorcycle with a small engine. Many models also have pedals. It uses little fuel, and is popular with young people.

## Chopper

An ordinary motorcycle with additional special parts is called a chopper. It is among the most exciting two-wheeled vehicles on the road.

# Cars

Cars first appeared on the streets over 120 years ago. Earlier models were slow and bulky, while modern cars are superfast with spacious yet agile bodies.

### Race car

Race cars are the fastest vehicles on four wheels, with powerful engines. They travel on specially made racetracks or across bumpy tracks through forests and deserts.

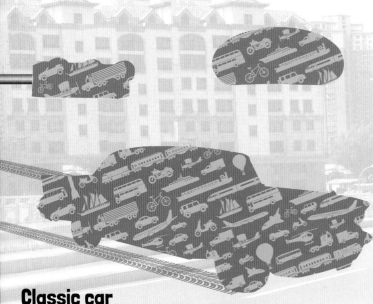

### Classic car

Classic cars include special models that have stayed popular over the years. Though not always the fastest or the biggest, it is often their great looks or durability that make them popular.

## FACT!

The Tucker was a classic American car made in 1948 that was powered by an engine originally used in a helicopter.

### Sedan

Sedans are comfortable cars with an enclosed trunk for luggage space. Some models are perfect as large family cars, while others are luxurious or high-performing sports sedans.

## Sport utility vehicle (SUV)

Designed to drive through rough terrain, an SUV is an automobile equipped with a powerful engine.

## Self-driving car

Driven by a computer, these cars have made it to the streets after years of testing. They have multiple cameras and sensors that observe the street, nearby vehicles, and hurdles.

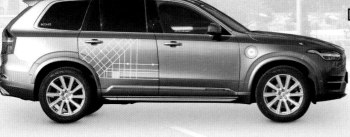

## Hatchback

This car gets its name from the door of the trunk at the car's rear. It's a sloping, hinged door (or hatch) that opens upward at the back of the car. The compact size and good luggage space make this car a favorite for city dwellers.

## Electric car

Electric cars are powered by chargeable, electric motors instead of engines that run on fossil fuels. They often have a simpler design compared to traditional cars.

# Buses

Buses are designed to carry a lot of people. A city bus takes short trips across town, while a coach bus can travel to another city, many miles away.

### Electric bus

Powered by electric cables, these buses are more eco-friendly than vehicles that run on fossil fuels. Equipped with chargeable batteries, these buses travel shorter distances in cities and towns without cables.

### Coach bus

These buses take passengers on long trips. They often have seats that lean back, television screens, and a bathroom.

### Articulated bus

Articulated buses are longer than regular buses. They are divided into two halves, connected by a bendable joint covered with rubber curtains.

### Double-decker bus

Some cities have double-decker buses for transporting people around town. With the old London Routemaster buses, passengers could hop on and off from the open back.

# Motor homes

Designed for long trips, motor homes are homes on wheels that come in various sizes. They are equipped with several utilities for life on the road.

### Camper van
These look like regular vans, but some people add beds in the back so they can be used as mini motor homes. They have luggage space and Wi-Fi for long distance travel.

### Recreational vehicle (RV)
RVs are popular for vacations across the country, especially in the US. They have household facilities like beds, a bathroom, and a kitchen.

### Luxury RV
Luxury RVs are large motor homes that can have lavish features, such as fireplaces, heated flooring, spacious bathrooms, and even home cinemas.

### Camper
Campers are compact motor homes for outdoor adventures. They come with built-in bunk beds, a working kitchen, and seating space.

# Trucks

Trucks are some of the longest, tallest, and widest vehicles on the road. While most of them are used for heavy pulling jobs, some are used in sports competitions.

## Pickup truck

Pickup trucks have a cab for carrying passengers and an open area in the back for transporting goods. On some pickups, the cab alone can be as big as a family car.

## Digger

Diggers have extra tools like a sharp blade or grab attached to them. These attachments allow them to do many difficult tasks easily.

## Excavator

Excavators have a long, clawlike attachment that can pick up and move heavy objects, such as scrap metal, rubble, or logs.

## Dump truck

Dump trucks transport loose loads, like sand, ice, snow, or coal. Also called tippers, they tilt upward to tip, or pour, out the material they carry.

## Bulldozer

Bulldozers do a lot of heavy-duty work. They have huge tires and an enormous blade to pick up and move bulky loads.

## FACT!

The world's longest monster truck, the Sin City Hustler, is about 32 ft (10 m) long. That's about half as long as a tennis court.

## Tanker

These trucks pull a trailer tank behind them. Sometimes the tanks are full of fuel, other times they contain liquids, such as milk or water.

## Monster truck

The wheels on monster trucks are taller than the trucks themselves. These trucks often race against each other on courses that contain large obstacles.

# Trains

Trains are one of the safest and most environmentally friendly ways to travel. The first trains were powered by steam. Now, they are either powered by diesel engines or by electricity.

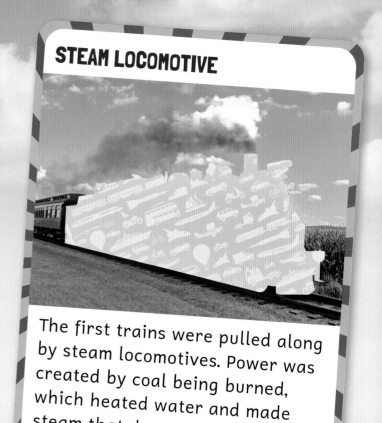

## STEAM LOCOMOTIVE

The first trains were pulled along by steam locomotives. Power was created by coal being burned, which heated water and made steam that drove the locomotive.

## FREIGHT TRAIN

These trains are used to transport freight (goods). They can be used to move products, such as food, coal, or cars.

## ELECTRIC TRAIN

Some trains move by using electricity from cables running above them. Electric trains are easier to maintain and don't produce smoke or fumes.

## HIGH-SPEED TRAIN

High-speed trains travel at speeds of over 160 mph (250 kph). Japan's *Shinkansen*, also called the bullet train due to its shape, was the first high-speed rail system in the world.

## LUXURY TRAIN

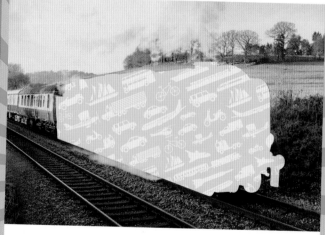

Luxury trains are richly decorated and have a lot to offer. The *Orient Express* was one of the most famous luxury trains in the world. It was in use from 1883 to 1977.

## TILTING TRAIN

Trains usually require straight tracks to run at high speeds. Tilting trains tilt inward at curves. This allows them to maintain their speed on tracks that curve.

# Subways

Mostly underground and out of sight, subways are among the busiest rail vehicles. Each day they transport millions of passengers to various destinations.

## New York subway

New York has one of the world's largest subway systems, with more than 460 stations. It runs 24 hours a day, 365 days a year, and Times Square is the busiest station.

## Hong Kong subway

Hong Kong's subway is thought to be the best in the world. Their system is advanced, cost-effective, and well planned.

## London Underground

The world's first subway system opened in London, England, in 1863. Steam trains were used on this subway for 100 years.

### DID YOU KNOW?

Tokyo's Shinjuku Station sees about 3.5 million passengers a day, making it the busiest station in the world.

## Tokyo subway

The subway system in Tokyo, Japan, is the busiest in the world. During early-morning rush hour, some subway cars are set aside for women and children.

# Cable cars

Often found in the mountains, cable cars are used to take people up and down hillsides. The car is pulled up and down by a cable.

### Chairlift
Chairlifts are common at ski resorts. They carry people up to the top of a snowy slope, and the passengers ski or snowboard back down to the bottom.

### Double-decker car
The Vanoise Express is the world's only double-decker cable car. Operating in the mountains of France, it carries 200 passengers on its two levels.

### Funicular
A funicular is a railroad cable network often powered by electricity. They can sometimes be found in cities, so that people don't have to climb up long, steep streets.

### Gondola lift
Gondolas are great for mountain sightseeing without having to climb steep and difficult slopes. Many gondolas have an observation deck at the end of the line.

# Trams and monorails

Trams are also known as streetcars. Some are powered by electricity in overhead wires, while others are pulled by a cable. Monorail trains travel on just one rail rather than two.

## SUSPENSION MONORAIL

The Schwebebahn, or suspension rail, is an upside-down electric monorail system in Wuppertal, Germany. The train has three sections and moves on tracks built on huge iron pillars.

## MAGLEV TRAIN

These trains "float" with the help of magnets and special tracks, using a technology called magnetic levitation. *Shanghai Maglev* is the world's fastest maglev train.

## AUTOMATED PEOPLE MOVER (APM)

APMs are fully automated, advanced rail systems. They're a bit like funiculars, which also don't have a driver, but APMs move along a flat surface instead of up slopes.

## STEAM TRAM

In the past, trams were powered by steam. Like a train, steam trams consisted of one or more cars pulled along by a small tram engine in the front.

## MONORAIL

Traveling on a single rail, monorail trains are usually used to take people short distances. They are often automatic, which means they do not need a driver.

## ELECTRIC TRAM

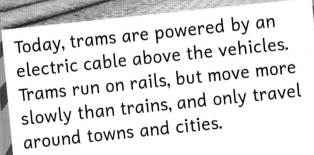

Today, trams are powered by an electric cable above the vehicles. Trams run on rails, but move more slowly than trains, and only travel around towns and cities.

# Boats

Boats come in all shapes and sizes. Besides transportation, they can be used for racing, exploration, or even just for a fun ride!

## Sailboat

Sailboats use sails to help them travel across oceans, rivers, and lakes. The wind pushes against the sail, and this moves the boat forward.

## Solar-powered boat

Solar panels attached to this boat convert the sun's energy into electricity. Although the boat cannot go very fast, it is quiet and nonpolluting.

## Kayak

A kayak is a light, narrow boat. A double paddle is used to move it through water. Kayaking is a popular water sport.

## Ferry

In many waterfront cities, a ferry is part of the transportation system. This boat can dock and leave quickly since it doesn't need to turn around.

# Ships

Ships are usually larger than boats. They operate in oceans and high seas, and are mainly designed to transport goods and people.

## Sailing ship
Hundreds of years ago, people traveled across the world's oceans in huge sailing ships to explore and trade with other countries.

## Container ship
This massive ship transports thousands of containers filled with all kinds of goods. The containers are as big as trucks.

## Icebreaker
An icebreaker ship has a specially shaped bow (front) that crushes ice as it travels across the ocean.

**DID YOU KNOW?**
The *Titanic* had a swimming pool, a barber shop, Turkish baths, and cafes for its first-class passengers.

## Cruise ship
These big ships are floating hotels that provide lavish trips around the world. The *Titanic* was one of the most luxurious ships of its day.

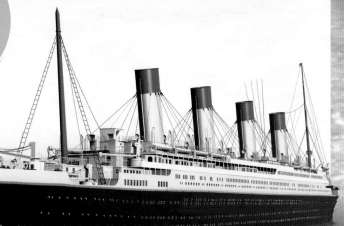

# Hovercraft

Hovercraft are very adaptable. Riding along on a bed of air, they can travel on water, land, ice, and sand.

### Electric hydrofoil

An electric hydrofoil is designed like a surfboard to glide above water. It uses chargeable batteries and a silent motor.

### Rescue hovercraft

Hovercraft are sometimes used on rescue missions. Because they ride on a bed of air, they can enter the water at any point and reach people in need quickly.

## FACT!

The hovercraft was invented by British electronic engineer Christopher Cockerell in the 1950s.

### Flyboard

A flyboard is attached to a jet ski through a hose. The high pressure water from the jet ski pushes the rider up into the air. The rider must balance to steer the craft.

### Hydrofoil

A hydrofoil uses "wings," called foils, to ride above the surface of the water. It can travel much faster than a traditional boat.

# Submarines

Submarines are vessels that transport people deep down into the ocean. Some make short trips underwater, others stay submerged for months at a time.

## Bathyscaphe

Bathyscaphes can dive deeper than a submarine. The *Trieste* bathyscaphe traveled more than 33,000 ft (10,000 m) underwater, setting a world record in 1960.

## Deep submergence rescue vehicle (DSRV)

DSRVs are large submarines built to assist and rescue the crews of other submarines. They can travel to great depths.

### DID YOU KNOW?

HM Submarine *Warspite* holds the record for the longest period a submarine crew has spent underwater: 111 days!

## Tourist submarine

Tourist submarines offer people a chance to see hidden underwater sights. They can also access the viewing deck on top, once it is above the water's surface.

## Military submarine

Used for military purposes, these submarines carry weapons. They remain in water for long periods of time without making much noise.

# Airplanes

For more than a century, people have been able to take to the sky and fly in airplanes. From light aircraft to large passenger planes, airplanes allow us to speed across the globe.

### Early plane

This airplane was built in Europe nearly 100 years ago and could carry just one person—the pilot. The plane was made out of wood and fabric.

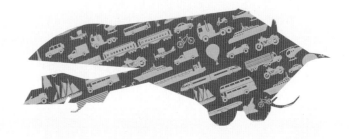

### Passenger plane

Also called airliners, passenger planes fly people from one place to another. The biggest passenger planes can hold over 800 people!

### Light aircraft

Small, light airplanes are useful for short trips. Light aircraft can be used by farmers to check their crops or by doctors to reach people who are sick or injured.

## Supersonic plane

Supersonic planes, such as the Concorde, can fly faster than the speed of sound. When the Concorde was in service, it could take passengers across the Atlantic Ocean quicker than any other passenger plane.

## Biplane

A biplane is an airplane with two wings. Although they are one of the oldest types of plane, biplanes are still flown today.

## Seaplane

What makes the seaplane different from others is that it has floats instead of wheels. This allows it to take off and land on oceans and lakes.

# Helicopters

Helicopters use rotor blades to fly through the air. On most helicopters, these large blades spin on the top of the aircraft, while smaller blades spin in the tail (back).

## Twin rotor

The twin (two) sets of large rotor blades on this helicopter allow it to carry very heavy loads. The twin blades spin in opposite directions.

## Air ambulance

An air ambulance is used to fly as quickly as possible to the scene of an accident. Seriously injured people are put in the ambulance and then flown to the hospital.

**DID YOU KNOW?**

A helicopter pilot has to use both hands and both feet to control the aircraft.

## Tourist helicopter

This helicopter flies tourists to places of natural beauty that are difficult to reach.

## Agricultural helicopter

These helicopters can perform large-scale agricultural tasks more efficiently than tractors. They are mostly used for crop dusting: spreading chemicals on crops to kill harmful insects.

## Gyrocopter

Unlike other helicopters, the rotary blades of a gyrocopter are not powered by an engine. It uses air to rotate the blades and fly. This lightweight aircraft is usually considered safer than most helicopters.

## Firefighting helicopter

Designed for firefighting, this helicopter has special equipment to help put out fires and conduct rescue missions. It can carry as much water as three fire engines.

## FACT!

The world's biggest helicopter is the Russian Mil Mi-26, which can carry up to 150 people.

# Balloons

The first people ever to leave the ground and fly up into the sky did so in a hot-air balloon. Today, balloons are used mostly for fun or for taking photographs of events on the ground.

### Solar balloon
These hot-air balloons are powered by energy from the sun. In good weather they can fly for longer periods than other balloons.

### Hot-air balloon
A hot-air balloon is filled with a gas called helium that rises up when heated and lifts the body of the balloon into the sky. Passengers travel in baskets under the balloon.

### Modern airship
A modern airship's body is made of fabric, and filled with helium gas. Some airships can remain in the air for days before landing back on the ground.

### Shaped balloon
Hot-air balloons come in all shapes and sizes, from cars and frogs to penguins and dragons. This one is shaped like an alarm clock.

# Gliders

Gliders are aircraft that do not have engines. They use rising air currents to glide in the sky, and are most commonly used in sports.

## Hang glider

The pilot of a hang glider uses rising pockets of warm air called thermals to lift it up into the sky. Cooler air allows the pilot to land the glider back on the ground.

## Paraglider

A paraglider is like a parachute that travels through the air. While some are pulled behind a car or a boat, others use a small motor to propel them across the sky.

# FACT!

Some ultralights can fly at over 170mph (274kph), which is faster than many light aircraft.

## Ultralight

An ultralight is made up of a simple fabric wing, a small engine, and a seat. Early ultralights were steered by the pilot swinging his or her body to the left or right.

## Modern glider

Gliders do not need an engine to fly. They are propelled into the air using another aircraft and then glide through the air.

# Spacecraft

Astronauts use spacecraft to travel into space to reach new places or dock (connect) with a space station.

## Mars Helicopter, Ingenuity

The *Ingenuity* was the first controlled aircraft on another planet. It weighed only 4 lbs (1.8 kg), as much as 10 apples. The aircraft hovered in the skies of Mars for about 55 seconds.

Pluto

## New Horizons

Almost the size of a grand piano, *New Horizons* was launched in 2006. Reaching its destination by 2015, it became the first spacecraft to orbit and explore the icy dwarf planet, Pluto.

## FACT!

The Russian astronaut Sergei Krikalev has spent a record-breaking total of 803 days in space.

## Cassini

*Cassini* was the first spacecraft to orbit Saturn. It collected data about the surface of the planet as well as its rings and moons.

## Soyuz

This series of carrier rockets has been operational in space since 1967. The spacecraft has been regularly redesigned for better performance.

# Rovers and satellites

Rovers are wheeled vehicles used to examine the surface of a planet or moon. Artificial satellites revolve around planets.

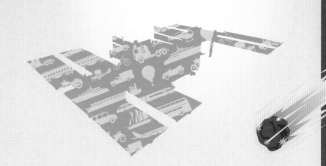

## International Space Station (ISS)

Bigger than a soccer field, the ISS is the largest artificial structure in space. Up to 12 astronauts can stay here to conduct experiments.

## Mir

Mir was the largest space station of its time. Astronauts from 12 countries visited Mir during its years in space.

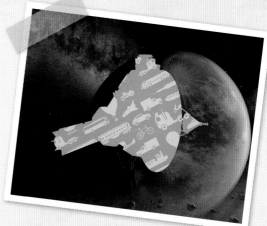

Mars

## Mars rovers

Mars rovers are remote control spacecraft sent to Mars to explore the planet's surface.

## Space probe

A space probe is an unmanned spacecraft used to explore objects in our solar system. It can orbit or land on objects in space.

# Vehicles of the future

Transportation is constantly changing to reduce the time, effort, and cost it takes to travel. Many technologies are being developed to make vehicles more useful and environmentally safe.

### Eco-friendly concept car

The stylish BMW i Vision Circular will be made of recyclable and renewable materials. It will have unique features, such as information projected onto the windshield.

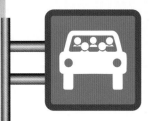

### Electric shuttle

Fully powered by electricity, the GEM e6 shuttle can comfortably seat up to 6 people. Safe and spacious, this vehicle could be the future of shared transportation service.

## FACT!

Some manufacturers make concept vehicles—one-of-a-kind models used to test advanced technology and special features.

## Low-noise aircraft

Planes flying faster than the speed of sound make a loud sonic boom noise. But NASA's X-59 plan should be a lot quieter. If successful, more planes will be allowed to fly at supersonic speed to reduce air-travel time.

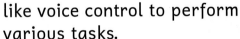

## Lunar rover

The Lunar Terrain Vehicle (LTV) would be the most advanced moon rover ever built. It will be able to transport both astronauts and cargo across the lunar surface.

## AI-powered concept car

The Toyota LQ will have an artificial intelligence (AI) agent named Yui that will communicate with the rider. Equipped with automated driving ability, the car will also use features like voice control to perform various tasks.

# On the road

## CHECKLIST

Use the stickers in the book to fill up the scene. Here's a list of vehicles that you might see on the road.

- [ ] Oxcart
- [ ] Tandem bike
- [ ] Chopper
- [ ] Sedan
- [ ] Camper
- [ ] Double-decker bus
- [ ] Bulldozer

# At sea

## CHECKLIST

Use the stickers in the book to fill up the scene. Here's a list of watercraft that you might see at sea.

- [ ] Sailing ship
- [ ] Kayak
- [ ] Electric hydrofoil
- [ ] Ferry
- [ ] Sailboat
- [ ] Flyboard
- [ ] Container ship

# In the air

Use the stickers in the book to fill up the scene. Here's a list of aircraft you might find up in the air.

☐ Air ambulance
☐ Hot-air balloon
☐ Supersonic plane
☐ Modern airship
☐ Gyrocopter
☐ Hang glider
☐ Light aircraft

# In space

## CHECKLIST

Use the stickers in this book to fill this scene. Here's a list of craft that have been in space.

- [ ] *Cassini*
- [ ] International Space Station (ISS)
- [ ] Soyuz
- [ ] Space probe
- [ ] Mir